Jane Cadwallader

Dr Domuch
and the Dinosaur Egg

Illustrated by Gustavo Mazali

CHAPTER 1: Dinosaurs

▶ **2** Ben, Pat and Sally were on their school holidays. They were at the Natural History Museum with their aunt and favourite person, Dr Maureen Domuch. Dr Domuch was the Museum Director but the children called her Aunt Mo.

Suddenly Sally saw a very big egg on a shelf. 'What's that, Aunt Mo?' she asked. 'It's a dinosaur egg,' said Dr Domuch. 'Would you like to go and see the dinosaurs?' 'Oh yes, please!' said all the children together.

▶ **3** The children looked at the dinosaurs in the museum. Dr Domuch told them, 'Some dinosaurs were very strong and fierce like Tyrannosaurus rex. They were carnivores. That means they ate meat.'

 'But not all dinosaurs were carnivores,' said
Dr Domuch. 'Some ate only grass and leaves
and plants. They were herbivores. Some of
these dinosaurs were small, most were big but some
were huge like Diplodocus. The biggest dinosaurs were
much bigger than any land animal that lives today.'

'What happened to the dinosaurs, Aunt Mo?' asked Sally. 'Why aren't there any dinosaurs now?' 'The weather changed but no one knows why,' answered Dr Domuch. 'Some scientists say it was because a meteorite hit the Earth.'

► **5** The children had lunch with Aunt Mo.
After lunch, all the children watched a video
about dinosaurs. Well, Pat and Ben watched the
video... Sally was busy doing something else!

▶ **6** That night, when everyone was in bed, Sally went downstairs to the kitchen. She turned on the oven very low and put the egg inside. 'Let's see what happens,' Sally thought, and then she went to bed too.

7 Sally got up very early the next morning and ran downstairs. There, in the oven, was A BABY DINOSAUR! It was green and white with a long neck and an even longer tail. It had two arms and two legs with a small head and very big eyes. Sally was very surprised and very happy!

8 Sally picked up the dinosaur and ran down to the
basement. 'You stay here and be quiet,' she said.
The dinosaur looked at her with its big eyes.
'I like you!' said Sally.

11

Sally ran upstairs. She woke up her brother Ben and her sister Pat. She told them, 'Last night I put the dinosaur egg in the oven and this morning there's a baby dinosaur. It's in the basement. Come and see!' 'YOU DID WHAT?!' asked Ben. 'WHAT'S IN THE BASEMENT?' asked Pat. 'Come and see!' said Sally again and they all ran downstairs to see the dinosaur.

10 They went to the museum. At first, Aunt Mo
was angry but then she was very excited. 'It's an
Oryctodromeus,' she said. 'Well, I'm calling it
Orry,' said Sally. 'Oryctodromeus... OK. Orry...
can run fast and it digs tunnels and it loves its
family!' said Dr Domuch. 'We can be its family,'
said Sally. 'No, we can't!' said Pat.

11 'Poor dinosaur,' said Pat. 'Its name is Orry!' said
Sally. 'OK. Sorry. Poor Orry!' said Pat. 'Think
about its future!' The children were sad.
They were sorry for Orry.

Look at that
funny animal!

Hmm... Just one foot long.

▶ 12 Ben had an idea! He said, 'What about finding an island where Orry can live? The island must have plants and water but it mustn't have people or fierce animals. Come on! Let's look on the Internet!' Dr Domuch said, 'What a good idea, Ben! And we can go to the island on my boat!'

▶ **13** Dr Domuch, the three children and Orry went to a village by the sea. Dr Domuch's boat was there. They took pasta, rice, eggs and a big bottle of water to the boat. They took salad and vegetables and a big piece of watermelon for Orry too! Finally they were ready!

▶ **14** They sailed for many days. They saw sea birds and flying fish and dolphins and big sharks. One day they even saw a whale. Finally they saw the island. It had a mountain and a forest and a beach with white sand.

'Hurrah! Hurrah!' shouted Pat and Ben but Sally
was quiet. She was a little sad because she knew
it was nearly time to say goodbye to Orry.

15 Dr Domuch, the children and Orry walked around the island. They found a river and a waterfall and a lake. 'It's perfect!' said Ben.

Suddenly, a coconut fell on
their heads... then another and
another and another! 'Oops!
Be careful! What's that?' asked
Dr Domuch.

▶ **16** They looked up and they saw a man in the tree.
'Go away!' said the man. 'This is MY island!'
'Please, don't be angry,' said Dr Domuch.
'We are only visiting your island.'

The man came down and talked to them. He told them his name was Harry. He told them about his life on the island. He showed them his house and they had lunch with him. They ate fish and bananas and pineapple. They drank mango juice and coconut milk. Everyone was happy.

CHAPTER 4: A new pet for Harry

▶ **17** Sally asked Harry, 'Are you happy here?'
Harry answered, 'Yes... but sometimes I'm sad.'
'Oh,' said Sally. 'Would you like a pet?'
'Oh yes!' said Harry. 'Have you got a puppy or a kitten or a parrot?'
'Well...' said Dr Domuch slowly. 'Sally, go and find Orry.'

18 Harry looked at Orry. He was very
surprised. 'But that's a DINOSAUR!' he said.
'Yes,' said Dr Domuch. 'But Orry is a very
good and very friendly dinosaur!
That's why we came to the island.
We brought Orry here to live.'
Harry looked at Orry again and said,
'Well, he's very
sweet...'

▶ **19** It was time for Dr Domuch, Pat, Ben and Sally
to go home. 'Do you think Orry is happy?' asked
Sally. 'Yes!' said Pat. 'Look at him!'
and they all smiled and waved goodbye.

It was difficult to see who was happier,
Harry or Orry!

▶ **20** Orry and Harry's song

▶ **21** Karaoke music

Activity Pages

1 **Read and write T (true) or F (false).**

1 A carnivore eats meat. ☐

2 All dinosaurs were carnivores. ☐

3 All dinosaurs were very big. ☐

4 Dinosaurs disappeared because
the weather changed. ☐

5 Maybe the weather changed
because a meteorite hit the Earth. ☐

6 Dinosaurs laid eggs. ☐

2 **What do you think? Choose and colour the star.**

1 Sally took Orry to the basement because…
☆ she wanted to hide him.
☆ he didn't like the kitchen.
☆ he was very big.

2 Aunt Mo was angry because…
☆ she didn't like dinosaurs.
☆ Sally took the egg without asking her.
☆ the children went to see her.

3 They take Orry to an island because…
☆ there are lots of vegetables.
☆ he likes digging in the sand.
☆ there aren't any people to look at him.

3 **What are these? Write. Number them in the order they appear in the story.**

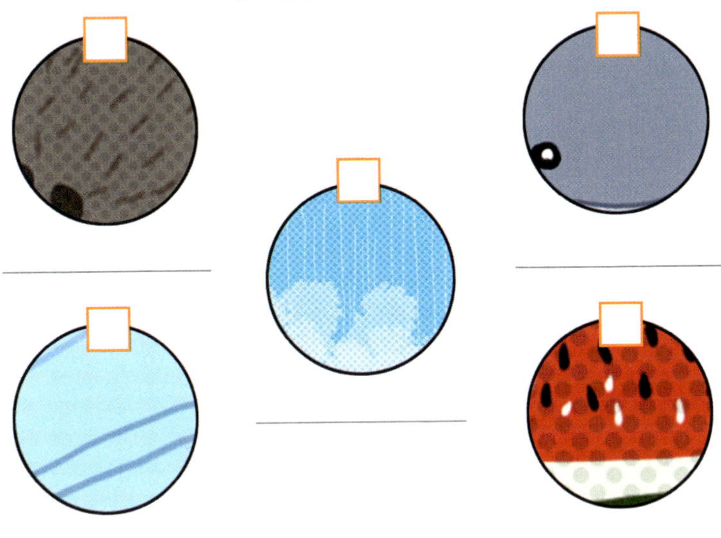

4 **Write the names of the characters. Match them with what they say.**

 A

 B

 C

 D

'Would you like a pet?'   'Go and find Orry!'

'Look at him!'   'He's very sweet!'

5 Reorder the letters to write the verbs.
Match the verbs to the pictures and past forms.

pcki pu

1 _____________

aet

2 _____________

tlel

3 _____________

sial

4 _____________

rnu

5 _____________

simel

6 _____________

ran

sailed

smiled

ate

told

picked up

6 Order the past verbs from activity 5.

Regular past verbs   **Irregular past verbs**

_____________   _____________

_____________   _____________

_____________   _____________

7 Use the verbs from activity 5 and *said* and *watched* to fill the gaps in the song. Count the numbers of letters to help. Listen to check and sing along.

Orry and Harry
1 _ _ _ _ _ _ their boat
And 2 _ _ _ _ _ _ _ the dolphins
In the sea.
They 3 _ _ _ _ stories
Under the stars
And 4 _ _ _ mangoes
For their tea.

Orry and Harry
5 _ _ _ on the beach
And 6 _ _ _ _ _ _ _ _ coconuts
Under the tree
And Harry often
7 _ _ _ _ _ _ and 8 _ _ _ _
'We're so happy,
Orry and me!'

8 Draw a picture of Orry and Harry on the island. Write a sentence about them.

____

____

9 Do you like the story? Draw your face.

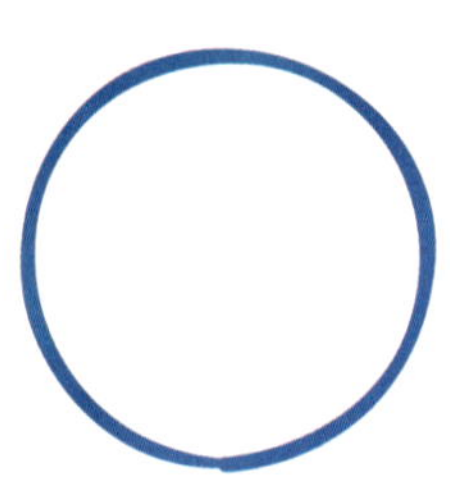

 = I love the story!

= I like the story.

 = I quite like the story.

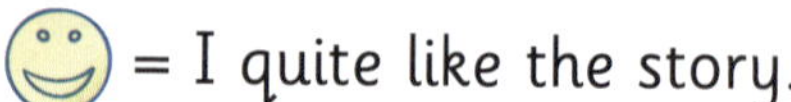 = I don't like the story.